Hello, Family Members,

Learning to read is one of the most im of early childhood. **Hello Reader!** bo children become skilled readers wh⊾ readers learn to read by remembering frequently used words like "the," "is," and "and"; by using phonics skills to decode new words; and by interpreting picture and text clues. These books provide both the stories children enjoy and the structure they need to read fluently and independently. Here are suggestions for helping your child *before*, *during*, and *after* reading:

Before

- Look at the cover and pictures and have your child predict what the story is about.
- Read the story to your child.
- Encourage your child to chime in with familiar words and phrases.
- Echo read with your child by reading a line first and having your child read it after you do.

During

- Have your child think about a word he or she does not recognize right away. Provide hints such as "Let's see if we know the sounds" and "Have we read other words like this one?"
- Encourage your child to use phonics skills to sound out new words.
- Provide the word for your child when more assistance is needed so that he or she does not struggle and the experience of reading with you is a positive one.
- Encourage your child to have fun by reading with a lot of expression . . . like an actor!

After

- Have your child keep lists of interesting and favorite words.
- Encourage your child to read the books over and over again. Have him or her read to brothers, sisters, grandparents, and even teddy bears. Repeated readings develop confidence in young readers.
- Talk about the stories. Ask and answer questions. Share ideas about the funniest and most interesting characters and events in the stories.

I do hope that you and your child enjoy this book.

—Francie Alexander
Reading Specialist,
Scholastic's Instructional Publishing Group

For Chris and Mim Galligan,
tree huggers and leaf lovers
—J. Marzollo

To the wheels under my cart:
Edie, Grace, and Gina
—J. Moffatt

The author and editors would like to thank Fred Gerber,
Queens Botanical Garden, for his expertise.

Cut-paper photography by Paul Dyer.

Go to www.scholastic.com for Web site information
on Scholastic authors and illustrators.

Text copyright © 1998 by Jean Marzollo.
Illustrations copyright © 1998 by Judith Moffatt.
All rights reserved. Published by Scholastic Inc.
SCHOLASTIC, HELLO READER! and CARTWHEEL BOOKS and associated
logos are trademarks and/or registered trademarks of Scholastic Inc.

Library of Congress Cataloging-in-Publication Data
Marzollo, Jean.
    I am a leaf / by Jean Marzollo; illustrated by Judith Moffatt.
        p.   cm.—(Hello reader! Science. Level 1)
    Summary: A simple introduction to the life cycle and functions of a leaf.
    ISBN 0-590-64120-4
    1. Leaves—Juvenile literature. [1. Leaves.] I. Moffatt, Judith, ill.
II. Title. III. Series.
QK649.M33   1998
581.4'8—dc21   98-5864
                                                                CIP
                                                                AC
12 11 10 9 8 7 6 5 4 3   8 9/9 0/0 01 02 03
                    Printed in the U.S.A.   23
                    First printing, September 1998

I Am a Leaf

by Jean Marzollo

Illustrated by Judith Moffatt

Hello Reader ! Science — Level 1

Cartwheel
·B·O·O·K·S· ®

SCHOLASTIC INC.

New York   Toronto   London   Auckland   Sydney

Hi!
I'm a leaf.
I live on a maple tree.
See the ladybug?
She's crawling on me.
It tickles!

Many leaves live in my tree.
We have a summer job.
We make tree food.

We make it from air
and sunlight.
Mm-m-m.
That sun feels good.

We also need water
to make tree food.
Rainwater goes into the soil.
It goes into the tree's roots.
It goes up the tree.
It flows into my veins.
My veins are like little pipes.

I mix sunlight, air, and water.
Then I add something green.
It's called chlorophyll
(KLOR-o-fill).

Chlorophyll is green.
It makes me green.

All summer long,
I have made tree food.
Once a caterpillar came by.
Nibble.
Nibble.
Nibble.
It ate a little hole in me.
But I still did my job.

Once a spider came by.
Busy.
Busy.
Busy.
It made a big web.
But I still did my job.

Once a squirrel jumped on me.
Boing!
Boing!
Boing!
It ran right over me!
But I still did my job.

Now fall has come.
My work is over.
My green goes away.
Now I am . . .

Red! Yellow! Orange!
It's party time!
All the leaves in my tree
are turning colors!
People *ooh* and *aah*.

The wind blows.
We break away.
We dance with the wind.
Whee-ee!
Gently, we land on the ground.

We rest.
Winter has come.
The forest is white with snow.
Some trees stay green.
They are called evergreens.

Slowly, leaves turn into soil.
The soil holds roots.
The soil holds water.
The soil holds animals
sleeping in dens.
Winter is over.
The soil warms.

Hi!
I'm a baby leaf.
Spring is here.
I'm the first bud to sprout
in my tree.

I'm growing fast.
Soon I'll get a job.
What will it be?
Mm-m-m.
That sun feels good.

MORE ABOUT LEAVES

Leaves come in many
sizes and shapes.
Most leaves make food
for their plants.
Which leaves are good
for people to eat?
(Salad leaves and spinach
leaves.)